Employee Onboarding

Employee Onboarding

The KISS Theory

A simple straightforward approach to personal and professional development.

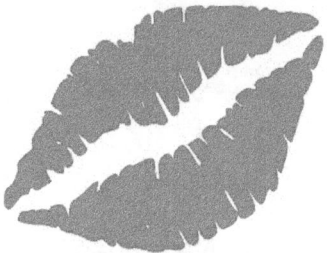

Jayne Finn

73 Greentree Drive, Suite 68, Dover, Delaware 19904
United States of America

116 Provost Street, New Glasgow, Nova Scotia, B2H 2P4
Canada

ISBN – 13: 978-1522702146
ISBN – 10: 1522702148

Your value doesn't decrease based on someone's inability to see your worth.

Unknown

To the Reader

I've been fascinated with the
KISS principle for several
years now. What is this KISS principle that's
got me so excited?

KISS principle

KISS stands for "Keep It Simple, Stupid" – a
design principle the U.S. Navy developed in
1960. Aircraft engineer Kelly Johnson (1910-
1990) has often been associated with the Kiss
principle. It basically means a majority of
systems work best if there is no complexity
behind them. Therefore, when it comes to
design, there should be no complexity
involved.

You may have noticed the 1+1 does not equal
two on the book cover. We are taught from
preschool that 1+1=2 a simple equation. Other
mathematical theories prove different that 1
+1 does not = 2. Personal development is
presented as a complex process. Once it is
broken down into simple steps there should
not be complexity involved.

As a teacher and facilitator I have searched for
way to develop a simpler way to approach
personal and professional development. I have
found it can start with a few moments a day of
mindful thoughts and simple awareness of self
and how we interact with others.

And, it was from this that the KISS theory came about. They're simple easy to read books that can provide insightful thoughts that can be used immediately. I have changed the "Keep It Simple Stupid" phrase, with "Keep It Strategically Simple." I certainly feel it gives a much better tone to get you to take action. Personal development begins with self-awareness; an awareness for us to improve and be a better version of who we are. When you reach the end of each chapter, you'll be greeted with practical illustrations, questions and a chance to write your thoughts down.

After all, I am a motivational quote enthusiast. And, as an adjunct instructor, I provide students with additional credits on tests if they memorize the quotes on the board. As an author, I issue you this challenge: memorize a quote or two for extra credit for your own self-discovery.

I am delighted to go on this journey with you.

Dedication and Acknowledgement

Dedicated to my husband, Terry Finn through personal sacrifice, and selflessness, bestowed the support and understanding without which this journey would not have been possible. I love you.

I also want to acknowledge our sons and daughter Todd, Tina, and Quentin whose personal development as adults have inspired me. My friend, Theresa Peaden who years ago encouraged me to pursue teaching and training (I thought she was crazy.) and provided me the opportunity to find my passion.

Simple Thoughts

"If you can't explain it to a six-year-old you don't understand it yourself."

Albert Einstein

"Genius is the ability to reduce the complicated to the simple."

C.W. Ceran

"We need to simplify life. Do you think grass thinks about who trod on it yesterday? No... It just continues to grow. And so should you. You cannot control who treads on you, but you do control your own growth. Don't ever let others inhibit you!"

Tony Curl

"Only those who have patience to do *simple* things perfectly ever acquire the skill to do difficult things easily."

James J. Corbett

"Life is really simple, but we insist on making it complicated."

Confucius

"Our life is frittered away by detail. Simplify, simplify."

Henry David Thoreau

"There is no greatness where there is not simplicity, goodness, and truth."

Leo Tolstoy

"Nature is pleased with simplicity. And nature is no dummy"

Isaac Newton

"If you will stay close to nature, to its simplicity, to the small things hardly noticeable, those things can unexpectedly become great and immeasurable."

Rainer Maria Rilke

"Nothing is more simple than greatness; indeed, to be simple is to be great."

Ralph Waldo Emerson

"I am not a genius; I am just curious. I ask many questions. and when the answer is simple, then God is answering."

Albert Einstein

"People often associate complexity with deeper meaning, when often after precious time has been lost, it is realized that simplicity is the key to everything."

Gary Hopkins

"To say more while saying less is the secret of being simple."

Dejan Stojanovic

"The truth is always simple. It's the mind that complicates it."

Joseph Rain

"My task is to simplify and then go deeper, making a commitment to what remains. That's what I've been after. To care and polish what remains till it glows and comes alive from loving care."

Sue Bender

"Human beings, viewed as behaving systems, are quite simple. The apparent complexity of our behavior over time is largely a reflection of the complexity of the environment in which we find ourselves."

Herbert A. Simon

"Simplicity is a kind of transparency in which subtle nuances can have outsize effects."

David Byrne

Wisdom is the highest strength; simplicity has intrinsic power."

Debasish Mridha M.D.

"Simplicity allows a measure of freedom which the complexities of modern life greedily consume freedom to think, to reflect, to create, to serve and be sincerely generous with our time and presence."

Mary Morrell

"It's the simplest things that can convey a message...."

Peter Cimino

"Here's to the moments when you realize the simple things are wonderful and enough."

Jill Badonsky

"That's been one of my mantras — focus and simplicity. Simple can be harder than complex: You have to work hard to get your thinking clean to make it simple. But it's worth it in the end because once you get there, you can move mountains. [BusinessWeek, May 25 1998]"

Steve Jobs

CONTENTS

PREFACE

Employee onboarding is essential to retaining top talent. An onboarding program does more than help orient new employees. It shapes how new employees relate to their organization. Implementing an employee onboarding program will shape the company culture while developing a highly qualified pool of talent.

> *The employer generally gets the employees he deserves.*
>
> *Walter Gilbey*

Chapter One:
Purpose of Onboarding

The purpose of onboarding is to help new hires transition into the roles at the company. When implemented correctly, onboarding will alleviate stress as it improves the culture of an organization. Employees who start well are more likely to stay at the company long-term. This will reduce turnover and save money in hiring and training costs.

Start-up Cost

Hiring new employees is expensive. Besides the recruiting costs and salary, there is a number of start-up costs associated with new hires.

Costs:

- **Salary**: This is the agreed upon pay rate.

- **Benefits**: This includes insurance, vacation pay, legal benefits, supplemental pay, and retirement. This is roughly .02 to .04 percent of the salary.

- **Miscellaneous**: These are the costs of training, rent, equipment, etc. This is .05 to 1.3 percent of the salary.

Onboarding can reduce the miscellaneous costs by quickly familiarizing employees with their position.

Anxiety

People naturally experience anxiety when they are placed in new situations. Taking a new job will automatically create stress. There is the stress of learning a new job and fitting in with the company's culture. Employees who are not properly oriented, both in their job and their surroundings, will remain stressed and anxious. Excessive stress will impede performance and increase company turnover.

Employee Turnover

Turnover is inconvenient and expensive. Replacing qualified employees requires more than onboarding costs. There are a number of factors to consider when calculating the cost of employee turnover.

Factors:

- **Exit costs**: This includes paperwork, exit interviews, knowledge, contacts, benefits etc.

- **Absence costs:** Company loses money in productivity, disruption, and possible overtime.

- **Recruitment:** The cost of advertising, recruiting, and screening candidates can be high.

- **Onboarding costs:** The cost associated with the hiring process.

There are very specific ways to calculate turnover. A basic method, however, is to estimate 50 percent to 200 percent of an individual salary.

Realistic Expectations

It is important to inform employees of the expectations placed on them from the beginning of their association with the organization. These expectations must be realistic. Not informing employees of all expectations, or making the expectation unrealistic, will hinder performance.

Expectations:

- **Company expectations:** The vision and mission of the company

- **Policies and procedures:** The company policies and procedures that everyone must follow

- **Housekeeping**: Informal rules and guidelines

- **Job description:** Expectations, training, and evaluation procedures of the individual's job

Practical Illustration

A small publishing firm had high turnover of 75 percent. Most employees left within a year, and very few people lasted five years. The company paid well, but people would not stay long. Eventually, the cost of turnover began to significantly cut into the profits of the organization. A consultant was hired to examine the problem.

The company lacked basic procedures. There was no orientation or onboarding process. New employees were hired and put to work without basic training. The CEO assumed existing employees would show new ones what to do, but they were too busy with their own work. New employees were scolded for their poor productivity, and most left for less stressful positions. Implementing a simple onboarding strategy reduced turnover by 55 percent within a year.

Personal Journal - *What are two or three points you can take from this chapter to enhance your companies employee onboarding experience?*

Encourage your people to be committed to a project rather than just be involved in it.

Richard Pratt

Chapter Two:
Introduction

There are a number of reasons to implement an onboarding program. Before this can be done, however, you need to understand exactly what onboarding involves and its importance to the success of the company. Exploring onboarding and its processes is essential to the success of any organization's onboarding program.

What Is Onboarding?

Onboarding is not easy to define. Some organizations limit it to a simple orientation process. Others go further to include company culture. Onboarding, however, is so much more. Onboarding is a systematic method that allows employers to hire the best employees and align them to the company vision. It will also provide employees with the necessary tools, help them assimilate, and speed up their training process.

Onboarding Affects:

- Hiring

- Aligning with company standards

- Accommodating employees with tools

- Cultural assimilation

- Accelerated training

The Importance of Onboarding

Employees typically "break even" 20 weeks after they begin working at a job. This means that their productivity equals what the company has invested in them. They begin to generate more value for the organization over time. Onboarding can improve the time that it takes for employees to become profitable once they are hired. This is accomplished on a functional level and a social level. Companies often focus on the functional level at the cost of the social. This can overwhelm employees and leave them feeling uncertain about whom to go to for help.

Examples:

- **Functional level**: Expectations, training, policies, procedures, etc.

- **Social level**: Networks, mentors, relationships

Making Employees Feel Welcome

When hiring new employees, it is not enough to just walk them through the office, hand them paperwork, and ask them to read manuals. You must make them feel welcome to alleviate anxiety and help them acclimate.

Ways to make employees welcome:

- **Contact the employee after he or she is hired**: This can be with a welcome letter or phone call.

- **Send information early**: Send the handbook and any paperwork that than be completed early.

- **Choose a mentor**: Assign someone to mentor the new hire.

- **Prepare for the first day**: Have everything ready for the new employee to begin work on the first day.

- **Have the new hire meet people the first day**: New hires should engage with their supervisors and mentors on day one.

- **Schedule lunch**: Schedule lunch with coworkers to introduce a new hire.

First Day Checklist

The first day for a new hire should be scheduled out. The first day will shape an employee's opinion of the organization and the people he or she works with. Do not have someone fill out paperwork and then sit alone while everyone else stays busy. Each company and industry will have a specific checklist, but there are a few basic guidelines.

Checklist:

- Greet the employee.

- Introduce the employee to his or her social network.

- Tour the facilities.

- Have lunch.

- Discuss all expectations

- Schedule the first week's training.

- Explain employee resources.

- Instruct employee on computer and telephone techniques.

- Conduct orientation session.

Practical Illustration

A manufacturing company was experiencing a time of growth. Employees were given a traditional orientation; however, without specific instructions, expensive miscommunications developed. Mistakes and errors occurred. Even with the new employees, productivity dropped 18 percent. The company instituted an onboarding program that focused on training new hires extensively. With better communication and training, productivity increased 10 percent and employee satisfaction improved.

Personal Journal - *What are two or three points you can take from this chapter to enhance your companies employee onboarding experience?*

Success always comes when preparation meets opportunity.

Henry Hartman

Chapter Three:
Onboarding Preparation

Every successful program demands preparation, and onboarding is no exception. While it is important to make employees feel welcome, the environment needs to remain professional. Before implementing an employee onboarding program, make sure that each person involved understands what is expected of him or her.

Professionalism

Onboarding needs to be a professional program. Companies frequently ignore onboarding responsibilities and simply assign the task of orienting a new hire to the least busy employee. This can cause confusion, impede the onboarding process, and give the impression that the company is not well run. It is essential that everyone involved in the onboarding program remain friendly and professional.

Professional activities:

- Make sure everyone knows that the new hire is coming.

- Choose someone to greet the new hire, and make sure he or she is on time.

- HR should have the paperwork prepared in advance.

- Designate a mentor ahead of time.

Clarity

Be clear about expectations with new hires and with everyone involved in the onboarding process. The new hire's expectations need to be communicated. There should also be clarity about who is responsible for the acclimation and training of the new hire. Each company and each position will have its own needs and responsibilities, which will determine the onboarding and training process. Determine everything you need to clarify before hiring a new employee.

Clarify:

- Goals: Clarify both company and personal goals.

- **Expectations:** Communicate expectations to the new hire, HR, and mentor.

- **Culture**: Describe the company culture.

Designating a Mentor

Mentoring is important to onboarding success. Designating the correct mentor can mean the difference between success and failure. The mentoring relationship will help determine how easily new hires transition into their roles at the company. Consider carefully who you choose to mentor new employees; do not just choose people at random. There are certain qualifications that all mentors need to have in order to be effective.

Qualifications:

- **Time:** Employees who are already overworked cannot effectively mentor another.

- **Training:** Is the employee qualified to teach someone else? Experience does not equal the ability to teach.

- **Role model:** Make sure that you choose a mentor who has qualities you would like to see in other employees.

After designating a mentor, monitor the relationship closely. If they do not work together well, you may need to designate another mentor.

Training

Onboarding should improve the training process. The people responsible for the training, however, must take the training seriously. Feedback is essential to the training process. Supervisors need to meet with new hires weekly to check on their performance and provide feedback. Those directly involved in the training process need to teach new hires and give them helpful feedback to improve performance.

Training Tips:

- **Train Tasks**: Teach employees the tasks associated with their positions.

- **Train Communication:** Train employees to recognize resources and to communicate their needs.

- **Provide Feedback**: Give consistent and encouraging feedback when training new hires.

Practical Illustration

The Time Clock Corporation attempted a new mentoring program to reduce a 75 percent turnover rate. The goal was to increase productivity and decrease turnover by 50 percent. The first review of the program showed a 15 percent reduction in turnover. While an improvement, the numbers show a need for improvement. A survey revealed that many mentors have little time to spend with new hires due to the demands of their own jobs.

Personal Journal - *What are two or three points you can take from this chapter to enhance your companies employee onboarding experience?*

In all planning you make a list and you set priorities.

Alan Lakein

Chapter Four:
Onboarding Checklist

One thing that will help onboarding go *smoothly is to create a checklist for each step* of the process. Keep in mind that the lists in this chapter provide a place to start. You will have to tailor each checklist to meet the needs of your own organization. The checklists will ensure that no part of the onboarding process ignored.

Pre-Arrival

Onboarding should begin before the new hire ever arrives at the organization. Preparing for a new employee requires a simple checklist.

Checklist:

- **Send welcome letter/packet:** This should be done two weeks before the start date if possible.

- **Prepare work area:** Have the work area ready as well as any necessary items nametags, parking permits etc.

- **Provide a contact:** Employees should be able to contact someone with questions before they begin work.

- **Schedule onboarding:** Schedule a start date, welcome, and orientation.

- **Inform others:** Let other employees know when the new hire is starting.

- **First week's checklist:** Work on the checklist for the first week.

Arrival

When new hires arrive, make them welcome and explain everything they need to know. Employees should not feel that their first day is a waste of time.

Checklist:

- **Welcome:** Greet the new hire; do not make him or her ask for you.

- **HR tasks:** Have the new hire meet with HR to complete any necessary paperwork.

- **Explain policies and procedures:** Provide a handbook and begin explaining basic policies and procedures.

- **Schedule:** Provide an orientation and training schedule.

- **Introduce:** Introduce peers and mentors as you tour the building.

- **Show workspace:** Show the new hire the prepared workspace, and make sure he or she has everything necessary to do the job.

First Week

The first week is when any housekeeping items are taken care of that is not attended to on the first day. It is also an important time to review the goals and activities of the new hire.

Checklist:

- **Review:** Go over the expectations and responsibilities of associated with the position.

- **Feedback:** Review and provide additional feedback. Ask for feedback about the onboarding.

- **Training:** Schedule necessary training and classes.

- **Inclusion:** Include the new hires in meetings.

- **Introductions:** Make any necessary introductions that did not occur on the first day.

- **Housekeeping:** Follow-up on any incomplete paperwork.

First Month

The first month should help the employee settle in easily. It is important not to become complacent when a new employee settles in quickly. Keep up with the first month's checklist to ensure that the onboarding is a success.

Checklist:

- **Clarify:** Continue to clarify roles and expectations.

- **Meet:** Meet weekly to give and receive feedback.

- **Enroll:** If necessary, enroll the new hire for any benefits.

- **Check training:** Make sure that the training is completed.

- **Evaluate:** Schedule a 30-day evaluation.

Practical Illustration

An expanding company needed to improve productivity by 20 percent in two quarters. Unfortunately, the growing number of new hires seems to be counterproductive to this goal. An onboarding process existed, but managers had control of the process. Checklists were created for each step of the process, and productivity improved 25 percent after two quarters.

Personal Journal - *What are two or three points you can take from this chapter to enhance your companies employee onboarding experience?*

In motivating people, you've got to engage their minds and their hearts.

Rupert Murdoch

Chapter Five:
Creating an Engaging Program

Any program you implement needs to be engaging. The purpose of employee onboarding is to engage employees from the beginning. Onboarding is more than simple checklists; it engages new hires in the company culture and promotes a highly functioning team. When onboarding is done correctly, employees are more engaged and productive.

Getting Off on the Right Track

Trust and communication are essential to employee engagement. Both trust and communication need to be established from the beginning. A common mistake that companies make is to force days of information into a few hours during orientation. It is not humanly possible for people to take in everything, and it is boring. Long, dull orientations give the wrong impression. They imply that the employer is not capable of communicating information well.

Classic orientations also erode trust because

employees are not treated like individuals, and those leading the orientation are not sincere. Orientations often have a disinterested HR employee simply read off information. There is no real connection with new hires, which does little to improve engagement.

Alternatives:

- **Break information down**: Give new employees information in portions they can keep up with, and schedule this transfer of information for the first week instead of the first day.

- **Build Relationships**: Have established employees who are passionate about the job and good with people take new hires through their orientation.

Role of Human Resources

The role of human resources will be unique to each organization. HR, however, has an important role in the onboarding process. HR representatives need to establish trust and communicate effectively with new hires.

Typical HR Roles:

- **Welcome**: Provide a welcome package and make individuals feel welcome.

- **Documentation:** Help employee's complete any and all necessary paperwork.

- **Policies:** Explain company policies and procedures.

- **Benefits:** Explain benefits and enroll new hires.

- **Tour:** Provide a tour of the company.

Role of Managers

Managers need to oversee the onboarding of new hires. They typically spend more time with employees than HR personnel, so it is important to establish a positive relationship from the beginning.

Typical Manager Roles:

- **Prepare**: Prepare the workstation, welcome, introductions, etc.

- **Schedule**: Create checklists and schedule training.

- **Communicate**: Explain roles and expectations to everyone.

- **Meet**: Connect with new hires and meet frequently to discuss their training.

- **Assign**: Choose a mentor and assign tasks to new hires.

Characteristics

There are certain characteristics that engaged employees share. As employees engage in the culture, they will exhibit these traits. Engagement is a sign that the onboarding program is successful and that new employees will stay for the long-term.

Basic Characteristics of Engagement:

- **Enjoy work:** Engaged employees enjoy their work. They are not simply working for a paycheck.

- **A good attitude:** They work towards the goals, and enjoy challenges and opportunities.

- **Go the extra mile:** Engaged employees do more than the minimum. They are committed to success.

Practical Illustration

The Good Song Company had a problem with retention. Employees seemed to leave shortly after they were trained. 50 percent left after the second year, and 20 percent left after the first year. Surveys showed that employees were not very engaged with the company. The basic orientation with HR lasted for four hours and consisted of reading the manual and signing documents. Managers were given the authority to onboard employees at their discretion. The onboarding process changed so that orientation with HR took place over a week. Managers turned in checklists every week. Over the next year, only 10 percent of the new hires left.

Personal Journal - *What are two or three points you can take from this chapter to enhance your companies employee onboarding experience?*

> *It's the people who follow through who excel.*
>
> **Mary Kay Ash**

Chapter Six:
Following Up with New Employees

Following up with new employees is essential to effective onboarding. Managers need to be involved with their new hires and determine whether or not any changes need to be made in their training process. Consistently meet with new employees and help them solve any problems along the way.

Initial Check in

The initial check in needs to be completed before the end of the employee's first month. Some managers try to check in after the first week. This is an opportunity to give and solicit feedback from new hires. The initial check in should focus on helping new hires become accustomed with the new environments.

Topics Covered:

- **Goals and progress:** Review the goals of the company and the employee's goals. Ask about progress, and cover material that the employee may not fully understand.

- **Discuss onboarding:** Make sure the employee feels welcome and that he or she has the tools necessary to succeed.

- **Offer help:** Solicit feedback and offer to help employees with their problems.

Following Up

Managers need to follow up with employees every 30 days for the first three months. Follow ups evaluate progress and check in to make sure that the employee's needs are being met. This is the time to address any confusion regarding company and employee expectations.

Topics Covered:

- **Mentor:** How helpful is the mentor?

- **Expectations:** Is the job what the employee was led to believe? Does he or she understand the job expectations?

- **Relationships**: How are relationships with peers and coworkers?

- **Inclusion**: Does the employee feel included in the process?

- **Work**: Is the workload too much? Are all of the tools available?

- **Feedback**: Ask about questions or suggestions.

Setting Schedules

Onboarding must be scheduled. Each time that you meet with a new hire, be prepared to provide new schedules. The checklists will help guide you in the scheduling process. Remember to allow individuals to develop at their own pace. Do not over schedule people. Schedule the next meeting each time you meet with an employee.

Schedule:

- Orientation

- Training for each week

- Meeting other people

- Follow ups

- Goals

- Evaluations

Mentor's Responsibility

Mentors are the key to a successful onboarding program. They need to take their role seriously and understand the responsibility of mentoring new hires.

Responsibility:

- Encourage the protégé.

- Act as a role model.

- Advise the protégé.

- Provide feedback.

- Assist in problem solving.

- Be trustworthy.

- Facilitate communication between new hire and other members of the organization.

Practical Illustration

A new sales firm was having trouble with its onboarding program. The CEO made sure that new hires were made welcome their first day and that managers and HR did everything to prepare for their arrival. Turnover was still at 60 percent and productivity needed to improve by 20 percent to reach company goals. Exit interviews revealed that no one checked in with new hires after their initial welcome. Some mentor relationships thrived while others did not. Frustration and confusion caused many employees to leave.

Checking in and follow-ups were added to

managers' responsibilities. Training was scheduled better, and employee concerns were addressed before they became serious problems. After the first quarter, turnover dropped 25 percent and productivity increased 30 percent.

Personal Journal - *What are two or three points you can take from this chapter to enhance your companies employee onboarding experience?*

An employee's motivation is a direct result of the sum of interactions with his or her manager.

Bob Nelson

Chapter Seven:
Setting Expectations

We have already established that setting and clarifying employee expectations is an important part of the onboarding process. Requirements and expectations need to be established from the beginning. New employees should not be surprised once they begin work. Set expectations and use them to evaluate progress.

Defining Requirements

Each position will have its own set of requirements. Requirements are more than a set of skills; they include everything necessary to perform a job.

Requirements:

- **Skills**: Abilities necessary to do the job

- **Experience**: Experience necessary to do the job

- **Education**: Training and education to complete the task

- **Company culture**: Personal and company values align

- **Behavior**: Attitude and behaviors necessary to be successful

Identifying Opportunities for Improvement and Growth

Meetings and evaluations allow managers to identify opportunities for improvement and for growth. In order to meet expectations, employees need to understand them. Any expectations or requirements that are not met should be seen as opportunities for improvement. Coach employees about ways they can improve.

Employees who do well may have opportunities for growth. These opportunities may involve additional tasks and changes to their expectations or job requirements. Any changes that accompany growth need to be explained to the employee, and assistance needs to be given.

Setting Verbal Expectations

Setting expectations verbally is a way to personally connect with employees. This allows managers to address any questions that employees may have concerning the expectations. Verbal communication, however, does need to be documented for HR purposes. You may want employees to sign that they understand the expectations that you express verbally. This is the only way for them to be legally accountable.

Putting It in Writing

Expectations should be put in writing. Begin with a basic job description. Job descriptions should be crafted before a position is filled so that employees know what is expected of them. Any changes to the job description need to be updated in writing.

Other expectations to put in writing:

- Evaluations
- Reviews
- Action plans
- Policies
- Corrective actions

Practical Illustration

A manager's department staff cannot reach their sales expectations. The manager tells the employees their individual goals every day, but they seem to ignore him. He is 20 percent off budget. Another manager advised that he documented the personal goals and had employees sign them at the beginning and end of each day. The employees took more responsibility in their performance and pride in meeting their goals. By the end of the quarter, the manager made budget.

Personal Journal - *What are two or three points you can take from this chapter to enhance your companies employee onboarding experience?*

*That which does
not destroy
strengthens.*

Nietzsche

Chapter Eight:
Resiliency and Flexibility

Resiliency and flexibility are important to success. People will make mistakes and no program is perfect, but reacting resiliently and learning to be flexible will eventually strengthen employees and the company. There are five steps to resiliency and flexibility. Managers, mentors, and employees need to take advantage of these steps.

What Is Resiliency?

Resilience is the ability to bounce back or keep going in times of stress or difficulty. Some people are more naturally resilient than others. Stress can take its toll on the physical and mental health of individuals. This can impede work performance. Greater resiliency will keep productivity from decreasing in times of stress.

Why Is It Important?

A new job is stressful. Employees need to be resilient in order to transition quickly and become productive members of the workforce. Resiliency is also important when the company goes through times of change. Resilient employees will remain productive and help keep the company going throughout transitions. Fortunately, companies can help their employees become more resilient by focusing on the welfare of their staff and providing incentives to manage stress.

Five Steps

There are five steps that anyone can take to improve resiliency. These require changing one's mindset.

Five Steps:

- **Acceptance**: Accept that change and failure is inevitable and not lasting.

- **Be self-aware**: Pay attention to strengths and weaknesses and focus on strengths.

- **Embrace adversity**: Realize that adversity may benefit you.

- **Relationships**: Create a strong social network and actively listen to those around you.

- **Set goals**: Make personal goals and work towards them.

What is Flexibility?

Flexibility is important for employers and employees. Employers need to be flexible when it comes to when, where, and how work is done. Employees need to be flexible in their approach to work and life in general. Being flexible means not resisting inevitable changes. Flexibility is not passivity. It is being open to change in order to improve life and reduce stress.

Why Is It Important?

Flexibility is important to recruiting qualified talent. Employers who do not cling to traditional job requirements are able to attract and retain talent. Flexible individuals act with conviction instead of reacting to change. Employers and employees both benefit from flexibility. Company culture improves as employees reduce stress and employers retain top talent.

Five Steps

There are five steps anyone can take to become more flexible.

Five Steps:

- **Let go**: Release any attachment that is making you inflexible.

- **Relax**: Practice work and life balance and stop taking life too seriously.

- **Do not focus on being right**: Be willing to admit when you make mistakes.

- **Pick battles**: Stop fighting every change and go with the flow.

- **Support**: Gather feedback and support from friends to find out when you are not being flexible.

Practical Illustration

A training manager with 20 years of experience began having trouble with his new employees. He used the same techniques as always, but the new recruits seemed bored. They did not pay attention during his slide show presentations, and he caught some people texting as he read from the manual. The company instituted an onboarding program that would alter the way he trained. The first attempt was less successful than previous orientations, but the manager only attempted onboarding begrudgingly. He embraced the change for the second group of new hires and found that they were more engaged and willing to listen.

Personal Journal - *What are two or three points you can take from this chapter to enhance your companies employee onboarding experience?*

Great ability develops and reveals itself increasingly with every new assignment.

Baltasar Gracian

Chapter Nine:
Assigning Work

The way you assign work to employees is important to the onboarding process. Sometimes it is possible to involve employees in the projects they are assigned. New employees, however, will have less experience and will need more guidance. Using the most effective method will make the task of assigning work easier for you and your new hires.

General Principles

Generally, assigning work requires employers to communicate basic expectations of who, what, where, when, and why. These expectations must also include what the work is, the due date, and any steps and tools that are necessary to complete the work.

Types of assignments:

- **Suggestions**: These are low priority assignments and completely open to interpretation.

- **Requests**: These are less official and are slightly open to interpretation.

- **Orders**: These are direct and leave no room for interpretation.

The Dictatorial Approach

The dictatorial approach is simply giving orders. It is the fastest way to assign work, but also the least effective. It should only be used in emergencies, and you need to explain the importance of the assignment. Employers who rely on the dictatorial approach have poor job satisfaction among their employees and usually high turnover.

The Apple Picking Approach

The apple picking approach allows people to choose their tasks from a list. These tasks are not typically high priority, and it is important that all tasks have the same value to the organization. This approach is helpful when there is little time to meet and discuss assignments. The drawback to the apple picking approach is that it does not teach collaboration and teamwork. It is also important to make sure that there are more tasks than employees, so that the last to sign up is not stuck with unwanted assignments.

The Collaborative Approach

The collaborative approach involves team meetings. Employees collaborate on who should complete each task. The team has a say in the deadlines and objectives of each assignment. This is the most effective way to assign tasks because employees are involved in the process. It is, however, time consuming and should be reserved for important assignments. This approach also works better when a team is established.

Practical Illustration

A CEO used the dictatorial approach to assign tasks to employees. She does not like being questioned and does not allow people to determine their own tasks. As a result, some employees feel that they are assigned tasks that they are not capable of performing. Over a six-month period, half of the employees give notice. The CEO hires a new HR representative to assign tasks. He implements the different approaches. Morale improves among employees who do not have to work with the CEO.

Personal Journal - *What are two or three points you can take from this chapter to enhance your companies employee onboarding experience?*

> *Feedback is the breakfast of champions.*
>
> *Ken Blanchard*

Chapter Ten:
Providing Feedback

Every supervisor needs to learn how to give and receive feedback effectively. Feedback is more than evaluating performance or checking in; it is a valuable method of communication. Poorly delivered feedback can lead to dire consequences. When done correctly, however, feedback will strengthen relationships as it improves performance.

Characteristics of Good Feedback

There are basic characteristics that define good feedback. When delivering feedback, try to focus on the positive. This does not mean that you cannot be honest or deliver negative information, but do so in a respectful and constructive manner.

Characteristics:

- **Dialogue:** Encourage a dialogue, and address any questions or concerns. Do not lecture.

- **Factual**: Discuss the facts, and do not bring up impressions or rumors. Use evidence to make your case.

- **Focus**: Stay on the topic and avoid personal issues.

- **Be clear**: Make sure that the employee understands expectations and has the tools to meet expectations.

- **Be constructive**: Point out successes and ways to improve instead of every mistake.

- **Compromise**: Be willing to make compromises after listening to your employee's perspective.

Feedback Delivery Tools

There are several different tools to help deliver feedback. Individual situations will help determine the best method for delivering feedback.

Tools:

- **Meetings:** Face to face meeting allow you to discover the employee's response quickly, but some people are nervous about meeting with the boss.

- **Email:** It is difficult to read tone in email, and it is not effective for complex situations.

- **360-degree feedback:** This is a review from every level of the company.

- **Reviews:** A performance review is the traditional feedback method.

Informal Feedback

Informal feedback should occur regularly. Feedback is provided as it is needed, which establishes communication between employees and supervisors. Informal feedback does not usually require a paper trail unless there is some type of correction or commendation. Informal meetings and emails are ideal for informal feedback.

What It Addresses:

- Praise

- Correction

- Questions

Formal Feedback

Formal feedback is traditional feedback. It is often scheduled and includes a great deal of paperwork. Performance reviews and formal corrective actions are examples or formal feedback. Formal reviews are done to record progress and discover opportunities. Formal feedback usually leads to promotions or actions plans for improvement. Formal feedback is limited because it is not consistent and may surprise employees when it is the only feedback they are given.

Practical Illustration

The manager at a local bookstore hated annual reviews. People were typically shocked when they left with their reviews and she did not understand why. Performance typically did not improve after reviews. The employees typically ignored her and exhibited the same passive aggressive behavior she pointed out in their reviews. The owner was unhappy with the culture at the store and demanded that the manager provide informal feedback. The manager took a course and applied positive and consistent feedback. The atmosphere improved and the sales increased 20 percent.

Personal Journal - *What are two or three points you can take from this chapter to enhance your companies employee onboarding experience?*

Closing Thoughts

- **Bruce Barton**: The five steps in teaching an employee new skills are preparation, explanation, showing, observation, and supervision.

- **Charles Reade**: Sow a thought, and you reap an act. Sow an act, and you reap a habit. Sow a habit and you reap a character. Sow a character and you reap a destiny.

- **Henry Ford**: The man who thinks he can and the man who thinks he can't are both right.

- **Dee Hock**: If you don't understand that you work for your mislabeled subordinates, then you know nothing of leadership. You know only tyranny.

- **Plato**: The beginning is the most important part of work.

- **Dan Miller:** "If you want to know my identity, don't ask me what I do or where I work, rather ask me what I am doing to make my life meaningful or how I'm fulfilling my purpose in life."

- **Anonymous**: "If you work hard at your job you can make a living, but if you work hard on yourself you can make a fortune."

- **Dale Carnegie:** "Many people think that if they were only in some other place, or had some other job, they would be happy. Well, that is doubtful. So get as much happiness out of what you are doing as you can and don't put off being happy until some future date.".

- **E.M. Foster:** "We must be willing to let go of the life we have planned, so as to have the life that is waiting for us."

Additional Titles Available

At thousands of major online and offline bookstores and retailers worldwide.

<u>Visit</u>

<u>www.thekisstheory.com</u>

To your continued success!

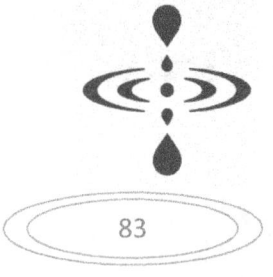

About the Author

The experience Jayne Finn, has goes back three decades, and involves training, coaching, and teaching. Jayne Finn, is a Certified Facilitator, Adjunct Instructor, and Entrepreneur. She's worked as a facilitator and consultant with various organizations including start-ups, community colleges and Fortune 100 and 500 companies. She is an advocate of lifelong learning. In her free time, Jayne enjoys long walks on the beach, collecting sea shells and photography. She graduated from North Carolina Wesleyan College with a degree in Accounting and holds Six Sigma Black Belt Certification.

With gratitude and appreciation.

www.ingramcontent.com/pod-product-compliance
Lightning Source LLC
Chambersburg PA
CBHW071609170526
45166CB00003B/1030